there's this girl

by

emilia thornrose

Wild Ink Publishing

A Wild Ink Publishing Publishing Original
wild-ink-publishing.com

Copyright © 2024 Emilia Thornrose
Edited by Ian Tan
Cover Design and Layout by Abigail Wild

ISBN: 978-1-958531-63-1

To my best friend.

You saw the darkest parts of me;

The broken pieces and all the rock bottoms

And you loved me anyway.

Thank you.

I love you.

table of contents

let's begin

There's this girl…
She's known by everyone
But only understood by some.
I happen to be one of those lucky few.
To her, I wouldn't sound so lucky.
She likes to divide herself -
One a wide-eyed child,
One a vengeful youth,
And one is free.
There's this girl…
Tired of the old
She decided to open
She wanted to be bold
She wrote down her mind
For others to share
To finally be transparent
Without having a care
So here is all of me
At last, whole and unbroken
~ *Here I am*

wonder

wonder

Wonder is a wide-eyed child's greatest virtue
Exploring cannot be helped.
But I guess the old saying is true;
Curiosity killed the cat.

I miss not caring

Sunshine in my hair

And bubble popping

I miss my hoping

Forehead kisses

And dandelion wishes

I miss her

I miss me

Before the hatred

Before the pain

Like I could live in a world

Feeling love again

~ Joy

In every accomplishment
In every loss
In every argument
In every joy
In every moment
I will love you
~ For as long as life goes on

You can leave
I may fade
I may grow older
I may break
But I'll still be here
~ *I am yours*

Partner in crime?
As long as you're my partner in time.
Today, Tomorrow, and Always?
Until the end of the line.
~ *Midnight promises*

Her laugh - a ringing sent to the Gods
It resonates as a reminder of the gift of her beloved soul
No other sound is as sweet
Only when it fades will my hearing be altered to the dull
gray sounds of earthly life
My greatest sorrow is the hollowed dread of that day.
~ An angels choir

Her hair;

Red curling locks

That blazed like the fire that burned in her heart

She was the morning sun

Full of life and a readied start

A battle cry

For any who dared to cross her path

She ran and played

As if she'd reduced her worries to ash

~ *Wildfire*

I wish we had time

Time to be everything we couldn't

To say all those things we shouldn't

I wish I could pause all the clocks

To live in those delicate moments with you.

It would be my most hopeful wish to share

My life, love, and daydreams with you

In those forbidden seconds.

But forever doesn't seem nearly long enough.

~ Lost in time

Her gaze - a tender love
And an innocence held close to her heart
She longed in his honeyed eyes
His melodious words promised that the skies
~ *Glancing*

Her gaze- a natural worldly wonder

A hurricane blue

A water I wouldn't mind drowning in

I loved and lost in her glance as she did the same

Just not in mine.

~ *Her*

She thinks she's weak.

She thinks she's stupid.

She thinks she's a burden.

I think she's strong.

I think she's proficient.

I think she's a blessing.

She thinks she's worthless,

But she couldn't mean more to me.

~ *She was my angel*

Her eyes;

Green and brown

Full of earth and all that grows

Looking on to the horizon

And all that she knows

Is there's nowhere else

That she'd rather coze

Then here with her

Where time feels like it slows

~ *Peace*

You were my wish
To have someone who knew me
To have someone that was true
Even better yet,
I had never expected to see
That you had wished for me too
~ *Samantha*

I would happily lay here for eternity
A forgiven sinner at your mercy
Patiently waiting forever
To love you like you've always deserved
~ Purgatory

Maybe we were meant for each other.
Maybe our souls traveled time and space,
Just to meet here now.
Maybe instead of believing in souls,
Maybe instead of studying the stars that they passed,
I'll just love you now.
~ *Soulmates in the moment*

Why can't you see how much I love you?

I know someone in your past

Told you that you were of little worth

And you consumed those words

As they were the only form of attention you received

But you mean so much more to me

You are worth so much earthly gold

That you could bring kingdoms to their knees

Begging and stricken with jealousy

With but just a gaze

You are worth so much time

That I would wait forever just to take your call

You are worth so much effort.

Give me your 3 a.m. cries and your smallest of victories.

I'll cherish each one.

I don't care about the drowsiness or the interrupted meetings.

They're absolutely meaningless when placed next to you.

For you, I'd stay awake just to watch you breathe

Because I know there was a time when you did not want to

Death let me have you for a while longer

And nothing could have ever meant more to me than that

~ *You are my miracle*

She keeps her joy under lock and key
No one's to know it exists
For if they knew it exists
It would take the shape of a target
~ *Target practice*

When you need her; the wonderous me
Look to the diamond shines of snow
and listen to the gentle honey bee
Watch the rushing summer waves
And inhale the fresh autumn breeze
Because for those of you who know
Unfortunately, I am no longer me.

~ *She is gone*

rage

rage

Blood gurgling.

Under your care;

I felt anger bubbling.

If you dare;

Proceed with caution.

We were never the stars
So perfectly aligned
We never saw eye to eye
We only ever went toe to toe
We fit like an accident
Something that shouldn't have been
You aimed and I took every blow
*~ **Destiny wasn't on my side***

I've never felt close to you.
I've never felt loved by you.
I was always the chore
The job
It was only a routine to you.
Why couldn't you see me?
Why wouldn't you hold me?
Why couldn't you love me?
~ *I don't know what I did to you.*

I call you mom.
But when I call you mom
I see someone who gave me life
I don't call you mother
If I called you mother
It would be when you learned to love me
~ *A mom isn't always a mother*

Hate is a strong word
But it's the right word
For when I hear your name
All I want to do is
Scream
~ You know who

Do I go after
The people I can't have
Because that's what
I think
I deserve?
Do I walk
This path
Because there Isn't
An end?

~ *Unattainable*

Loss on its own seems unbearable.

But is it worse

When they chose

To leave on their own?

Is there more pain?

Can there be more than unbearable?

~ *I miss you*

I miss our tea parties.

I miss listening to 80's rock together.

Goddammit,

I just miss you.

~ *Dad*

And still
After all this time
After all this pain
The only thing I could ask
Why?
~ *I need to know*

I gave you my soul

To have and to hold

You turned it black

And gave it back

It never did work

Quite right after that

~ *Him*

I felt empty

Around you

And I never

Want to feel that way

Again

~ *Mom*

I hate my way of thinking
Sometimes I blame you
For leaving me the way you did
And sometimes
I forget you're even gone
~January

Death is sleep
Death is the most peaceful rest
It is weightlessness
I am not afraid of it
But life...
That is a nightmare
That I'm terrified of living
~ *Life terrors*

You come to me in adulthood.

What am I supposed to do?

I don't need you now.

I needed you in youth.

~ *I was too little, you were too late*

Talking with you is
a time-traveling nightmare
Every time I do
I am a child
I am in a house
I haven't set foot in
In years
But I can still feel
The cuts on my feet
From eggshells
That have not left me
~ *I can't stand it*

I came into this world broken
Some pieces were jagged
Some weren't there, to begin with
But did you have to make it worse?
Did you have to smash those few pieces I had
Until I had nothing left?
Until I wasn't recognizable?
Until I barely felt human anymore?

~ *It was deliberate*

You hurt people.

You hurt me.

And because of you

Because of what you did

When you drank

I can't bring myself

To touch the thing

That destroyed my family

I know it is hard to quit

I know you'd rather feel nothing

Then the weight of reality

Believe me, I know.

But you are risking everything

For nothing.

~ Dear, dad

I tried to be pretty
I wanted to make you happy
But my stitches were slipping
And you never taught me how to sew
~ *I did my best*

Maybe it is because my dad left

Maybe it is because my mom chose someone else

But I am a jealous person

I am always scared that you will leave

I am always afraid that you will see my cracks and deem me broken

I have cracks and sometimes I am broken

But could you find it in your empathy to stay just a little longer?

~ I can't bear to be alone

I never loved you
Now as I look back on it
I think I was in love with the idea of love.
But never you.
I let you into my home
Into my mind
Into my body
I let you do as you please
I hoped that some way we could work
But when everything was over
When the final bell had rung
I was left open and broken
The windows shattered
My psyche snapped
My body burned
And you left me alone
With a smile that I can't forget
I haven't felt like me since.
~ 10th Grade

There are people in my life that I love so dearly

That it scares me

And

There are people in my life that I hate so devastatingly

That it's what I obsess over

~ *Contradictions*

Turns out
I'm pretty fucking easy to love.
Why was it
So hard for you to do?
~ *Dear, mom.*

I feel so much for you

I feel so much love

And so much anger

That no matter what I'm feeling

All I do

When I think about you

Is cry.

~ *Father*

I wasn't as protected as I should have been as a child

But now

I protect me

And someone would burn if they ever tried that with me

or any other woman again.

Let's see who would scald first.

~ *Anyone of you but certainly not me.*

relief

Relief

Relief is the growth after pain

It is the sun after lifelong rain

It is what I want to make

And the shape I want to take

I write because I can't say
I write because most don't listen
~ *The pen is my relief*

-60- there's this girl

Your smile wide
Full of life and laughter
And stories to tell
Your hands calloused
Full of love and loss
And memories to sell
Your eyes shine
The last light I've seen
Since our fond farewell
~ Melancholy ending

Sometimes we love someone
Who wasn't meant for the us now.
They were meant for an us years in the future
After we've grown
~ *The time traveler*

Never apologize
For simply just
Existing.
~ *Take up space*

All those years,

And everyone was hollow.

I love you

But I have to let you go.

~ *You're not mine*

If I spent my life
looking towards others
And their lives
And their achievements
I'd never have time
To look at my own
~ *Just a reminder*

Loving you
Was a mistake
But it taught me
To look for those signs
Read them and know them
And have the strength
To toss them aside
~ *Thank you*

I can't wait for the day
I look at me
And I can honestly say
I love you
~ *I'm waiting*

You will

Never

Have that power

Over me

Again.

~ I can't, I won't, I reuse.

My body will never tell you what my favorite flower is

Or how I want them more than only once a year

It won't tell you that I love to knit

But have never finished a single project

It will never show you that I hate sunrises

Or that every night I tell the stars goodnight before bed

Or how much I love horror movies

even though I always get too scared to sleep alone afterward

My body will never let you know my worst memories

My body will never share my deepest secrets

Or ever utter my most hopeful of wishes

You never seemed to understand that.

~ *I am not my body*

People will come and go.

Let them.

Keep going

~ *Don't slow down*

Acknowledge it.

Accept it.

Someone looked at you.

They saw your dreams

And felt your soul.

They held your broken pieces

And listened to your worst tendencies.

They knew you.

They. knew. you.

And they loved you anyway.

~ *Get over it.*

Maybe we never had forever

But I had all your midday snippets about your day

And your late-night calls about your fears

I knew you deeply

completely

And I'd take that year with you

Over a lifetime with anyone else

~ November 8th

I never trusted people.
I never liked them that much
But it was not because I did not want to
I want to be the kind of person
That puts their faith in people
Because I know what it is like when no one had faith in me
And maybe I get hurt a few times
But there will be a time when it fits
A time when someone needed it
And I was there for them
Someday
I may help someone
And it would be worth it
~ Have faith

Just because

I am different,

that does not

make me worthless.

~ You do not decide my worth.

Who cares if it is selfish?
Be selfish.
Be selfish and be happy
Nothing else should matter
~ *Don't listen to them.*

I am my own person

And you know what?

I'm pretty damn great

And trying my best to be better

You have no idea how long it took to get there.

~ *Growth*

one more before you go

Life is filled with ups and downs.
It's filled with beauty and pain.
I continue to grow from both experiences
And I never want to forget a single one.
They made me who I am.
If you got this far in the book,
From the bottom of my heart,
Thank you for getting to know me

Emilia Thornrose was born in December of the year 2000 in southeastern Kentucky. She grew up with a love of romance and fantasy. She began writing at thirteen and never looked back. She has written "Hope" in The Carnation Collection, and "The Imposters Game" in Tenpenny Dreadfuls: Tales as Hard as Nails. She is also the author of "There's This Girl". Her work is an extension of herself and serves the purpose of connection, to resonate with others. Everyone knows the feeling of being alone, misunderstood, or unappreciated. Emilia's work talks about the good days and the bad to remind readers they aren't alone and that no matter where they come from, they're seen, and they matter.